Vayu, The Wind

By Madhuri Pai and Rohini Nilekani

Illustrated by Rijuta Ghate

Library For All Ltd.

Library For All is an Australian not for profit organisation with a mission to make knowledge accessible to all via an innovative digital library solution. Visit us at libraryforall.org

Vayu, The Wind

This edition published 2022

Published by Library For All Ltd
Email: info@libraryforall.org
URL: libraryforall.org

Library For All gratefully acknowledges the contributions of all who made previous editions of this book possible.

www.africanstorybook.org

Original illustrations by Rijuta Ghate

Vayu, The Wind
Pai, Madhuri and Nilekani, Rohini
ISBN: 978-1-922918-04-8
SKU03032

Vayu, The Wind

I finish my hot, hot bath. My wet body feels so cool, cool, cool. What makes that happen?

Vayu, the wind!

The milk in my cup is too hot. But soon it is ready for me to sip. Who makes that happen?

Vayu, the wind!

The window curtains flutter
and gently brush my face.
Who makes it happen?

Vayu, the wind!

A bolt of lightning far away.
Black clouds moving my way.
Who makes that happen?

Vayu, the wind!

Branches sway and leaves tremble. Flowers gently fall. Who did it all?

Vayu, the wind!

We are playing far from the house. Yet I can smell the food mother is preparing. Who makes it happen?

Vayu, the wind!

A glass on a windowsill,
crashes to the ground.
I am glad I was not around.
Who broke the glass?

Vayu, the wind!

A whistle blows. A train rolls in. I cannot see it, but I hear its din. Who makes that happen?

Vayu, the wind!

Cannot be seen.
Cannot be heard.
Works without saying a word.
Who can it be?

Of course! The wind!

You can use these questions to talk about this book with your family, friends and teachers.

What did you learn from this book?

Describe this book in one word. Funny? Scary? Colourful? Interesting?

How did this book make you feel when you finished reading it?

What was your favourite part of this book?

download our reader app
getlibraryforall.org

About the contributors

Library For All works with authors and illustrators from around the world to develop diverse, relevant, high quality stories for young readers. Visit libraryforall.org for the latest news on writers' workshop events, submission guidelines and other creative opportunities.

Did you enjoy this book?

We have hundreds more expertly curated original stories to choose from.

We work in partnership with authors, educators, cultural advisors, governments and NGOs to bring the joy of reading to children everywhere.

Did you know?

We create global impact in these fields by embracing the United Nations Sustainable Development Goals.

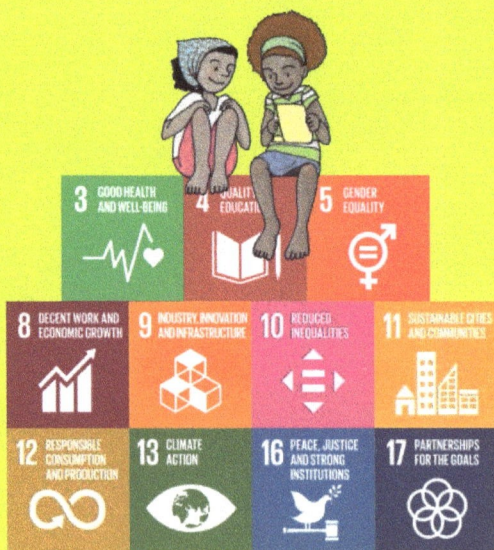